SKYE FOR BEGINNE

Besley

NEIL WILSON PUBLISHING
Glasgow · Scotland

D0525061

Text © Rupert Besley, 1999
All illustrations © Rupert Besley, 1999
The author has established his moral right to be identi-
fied as the author and illustrator of this work.
All rights reserved.

Published by Neil Wilson Publishing Ltd
303a Pentagon Centre, 36 Washington Street
Glasgow G3 8AZ
Tel: 0141-221-1117
Fax: 0141-221-5363
e-mail: nwp@cqm.co.uk
http://www.nwp.co.uk/

*To write about somewhere that is not your home or
birth-place is always risky, especially where humour is
involved. I can only hope that any jokes that may
appear in the text are seen to be, as intended, at the
expense of the ignorant visitor, such as myself, and not
the long-suffering residents who put up with us.
Sincerest thanks are due to the many kind people of
Skye and its surrounding parts who have given us
quite wonderful holidays.*

A catalogue record for this book is available from
the British Library
ISBN 1-897784-76-7

Typeset in 9/10pt Bodoni
Printed in the UAE

1 3 5 7 9 10 8 6 4 2

Contents

IN THE BEGINNING

Skye was first discovered in 1773. The man responsible was Dr Johnson, an opinionated Englishman who toured the Highlands, sounding off about the locals and disappearing before the bill came. His example has inspired countless followers down the years.

With Boswell in tow, Johnson landed at Armadale in early September. Their progress took them on to Broadford, Corriechatachan, Dunvegan and Gesto, then back via Talisker and Ullinish. As the author of a famous dictionary, Johnson was used to doing things in alphabetical order.

Samuel Johnson was famous as a wit, a certain amount of which may have been lost on his hosts. His *Journey to the Western Islands of Scotland* has been read, re-read and read again more slowly by successive generations, each unable to get the jokes.

To which, sir, it might hardly be necessary for me to add, without fear of contradiction, lest I digress, that in such barren ground and amid such barbarian practices as are here to be witnessed upon the Island of Sky, yonder fearsome cataract notwithstanding, it would appear that nolens volens such quiddities of Nature that do perforce obtain within her midst, countermanding the sullen disposition of the Gael whose attenuations in such a clime blather blather blah blah...

Dr Johnson delivering one of his famous witty one-liners

Getting There

FIRST get to Scotland. For many, if not most, that means getting into the car and belting up the M6 with boats, bikes and contents of the garden-shed variously attached. Some go one better by taking the shed, having given it wheels and an assortment of witty pennants and stickers to amuse the tailback behind.

Scotland begins at Gretna and the Highlands begin by Loch Lomond – just by the Gents in Duck Bay. Far behind are Croydon, Crawley, Watford and Penge – safely on another planet. Ahead lie Rannoch Moor, Glencoe and Skye. Things start to look up.

Fly . Drive

ROWED TO THE ISLES

The best-known way over to Skye is by open rowing-boat from South Uist. It takes about 12 hours and be prepared to strike up with cheering shanties when the sea gets rough. Dressing as an Irish maid is optional.

There are other ways, except in winter (ferry time-tables being based on the premise that most people's cars will be snowed into their garages from October to March).

Fly-Drive is a popular means of reaching the Highlands. Rail- and air-links exist with Inverness (Skye-Train) and from Fort William there is the Jacobite Steam Train, which is some age for a train.

Alternatively:

❑ a regular year-round ferry service operates into Uig from Tarbert in Harris and Lochmaddy in North Uist. The nimble-footed can try Island Hopscotch, jumping ferries as appropriate.

❑ a shorter crossing is offered by the sturdy vessel which plies between Raasay and Sconser throughout the week, but not on Sundays, Heaven forbid.

❑ the much-loved car-ferry (people queued for it from miles around) from Kyle of Lochalsh to Kyleakin has sadly been withdrawn on Government orders. However, the narrows here are just passable with care by amphibious vehicle.

□ swimming the Kyle of Lochalsh takes 18 min 15 secs, but not with luggage.

□ a wonderful crossing, deservedly popular, is the family-run service from Glenelg to Kylerhea (via Balmacara and Dornie when the tide is at its strongest). The journey (summer only) takes just 5 minutes, seals, otters, dolphins, porpoises and sea-serpents permitting.

□ the attractive route from Mallaig to Armadale is also seasonally restricted. Roll-on/roll-off facilities are available to vehicles from April to October, but in winter months are limited to foot-passengers only.

□ a less frequent service, but no less enjoyable for that, is provided by the cruise ships *Radisson Diamond* and *Radisson Flower of Song*, which arrive in Loch Dunvegan from the Isle of Man at least once a year in the summer. These are modern catamarans, equipped with every luxury, but one heck of a long wait if you miss your sailing.

□ and then there is that bridge.

Roll·on , roll·off

Lightening the load

THAT BRIDGE

Or, more accurately, those bridges.

Built to improve communications between the Isle of Skye and the Sheriff Court in Dingwall, the bridge was opened in 1995.

It has its admirers, who gather frequently to celebrate the achievement with banner-waving and colourful parades. On the former island of Skye, however, opinion as to the bridge is sharply divided. 1% like it; 99% don't.

The prices charged and the pockets this fortune is going into are the chief causes of local indignation. A glance down the list of names of those charged with non-payment (Margaret Thatcher, Saddam Hussein, Michael Forsyth...) makes it clear that discontent with the tolls is not confined solely to the people of Skye.

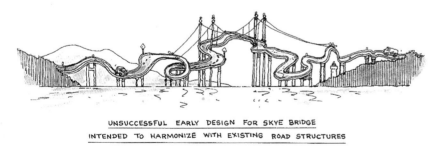

UNSUCCESSFUL EARLY DESIGN FOR SKYE BRIDGE
INTENDED TO HARMONIZE WITH EXISTING ROAD STRUCTURES

Geography

BLUE SKYE

O N the same latitude as Hudson Bay, Labrador and Tomsk in Siberia, Skye should be buried under several feet of snow for much of the year. Instead the Gulf Stream delivers a steady blast of sub-tropical heat, in which the island swelters. It's a pretty merciless sun that beats down on the coral beaches of Skye, obliging visitors to scurry back to the palm trees of Plockton in search of shade.

Other parts of Scotland can be notably chilly – not for nothing does Nature equip Shetland ponies and Scotch eggs with that extra layer of insulation. But not Skye.

Sometimes, true, the mountain tops are hidden from view, but the billows here are not mist or cloud in the ordinary sense but hot steam rising up from the glens.

For brilliant colours and clarity of light, autumn is a good time to be in Skye. That's when crisp mornings awaken the senses and fiery sunsets inflame the western skies in a blaze of spectacular glory. And sometimes it rains.

Tourist Tip: Plan well ahead – choose a week when the weather's going to be fine.

You should have been here last week –

ICES

SCOTTISH WEATHER

GEOLOGY

Put simply, Skye is noted for the plagioclase gabbro of
The Cuillin, on the northern flank of which lateral injec-
tions of viscous magma have resulted in basaltic flows
interdigitated with rhyolitic lavas, pyroclastic tuffs and
agglomerates, combining as trachytes with porphyritic
andesites.

Actually, geology is not that complicated – not if you
have a PhD in Glaciomorphology, a large dictionary and
a well-sharpened hammer (for settling arguments).

Volcanic dykes, intrusive granites, plugs and sills –
with its neat examples of almost every known part of a
geology degree course, Skye is heaven to geologists.
Easter is the time for field trips, when Skye becomes the
stamping-ground of student-parties brought over to
stare at funny rocks and to experience for themselves
the effects of glaciation.

13

ROCK BOTTOM

Some of the oldest exposed rocks in the world are in Sleat: Lewisian Gneiss is older than the hills.

Up in Strath and bits of Trotternish these ancient rocks are coyly clad in younger limestones. Hence the change from acid bogland to the lush crofts of Torrin and Staffin, where the grass is sweet, flowers abound and you can't hear yourself think over the rasp of corncrakes in the meadow.

Spread over the rest of Skye are the various layers of volcanic vomit spewed out by successive eruptions 60 to 50-odd million years ago. Along came the Ice Ages to scoop out lochs and straighten up the glens. The ice melted, land slipped and the basalt cracked. Bits broke off the edge to slither to the sea. The Storr Rocks and the Quiraing were born, much to the delight of the Tourist Board. Simple, really.

volcanic dykes

intrusive granites

glacial erotics

'SGURR : a sharp rock '

PLACE-NAMES

Skye takes its name from the Norse *skuyo*, which means 'cloud'. Or it comes from the Gaelic *sgiath*, meaning 'wing'. Or *sgeir*, 'a sea-rock'. Or...

Derivation of place-names is a tricky business at the best of times, and especially so on Skye with its chequered past. Skye has always been overrun by foreigners. Once it was hairy-kneed Vikings, with names like Saucy Mary, Magnus Barelegs and Olav the Red. Nowadays such folk tend to come from a little further south, Germany and Italy mostly.

All have left their mark on the landscape and the map of Skye reads like a visitor's book of past invaders. Norse names are interesting. The ending -shadder (as in Ellishadder, Marishader, Herishader) means ' a high grazing-ground or shieling'. Shulishader, by Portree, is where gannets were taken to be fed. Broadford comes from the Norse *breida-fjord*, meaning 'broad ford'.

Most names on Skye are used twice, at opposite ends of the island, in order to lose the tourists. Skye has at least two Uigs, two Idrigills, two Carbosts, two Borves, two Kilmuirs, two Oronsays, two Boreraigs, two Ardmores, two Loch Eishorts, two Beinns na Caillich, three Loch Fadas, three Swordales, three Lyndales, several Totes and Beinns Bhuidhe and Bhreac beyond counting. Probably more, if you look.

The Tour

PENINSULAS

HEAVILY indented by sea-lochs, Skye divides into six distinctive areas – Sleat, Strath, Trotternish, Waternish, Duirinish and Minginish. These in turn are generally grouped into two main areas: Sortofmiddleish and Milesoutthereish. Residents at the extremities of Skye have unrivalled scenery, but they are miles from anywhere, whereas centrally placed Portree is equally miles from everywhere.

First-time visitors to Skye invariably slip up on jour-ney-times. Distances can be up to ten times that which is first imagined. Always allow for the probability that a camper-van has clipped the end off your sign-post, removing its final digit.

Armadale to Staffin is about 300 miles (or 850 there and back). For the trip from Broadford to Elgol allow several days, some of which will be spent in reversing your vehicle to the nearest passing-place. The more timid will in due course find themselves back at Kylerhea instead. Reversing round Skye is a recognised form of visitor travel.

MONDAY MORNING IN SLEAT

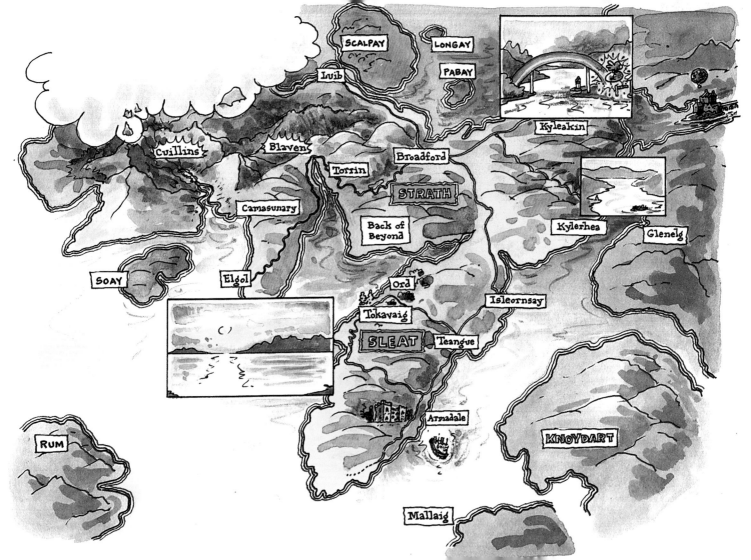

SLEAT

Sleite/Sleat, the Garden of Skye, is not all rockeries, rose-beds and neat little rows of fruit 'n veg. Indeed, you'd be hard put to find a decent gnome or line of radishes within the whole peninsula.

Dun Sgathaich/Dunscaith, 'the castle of gloom', is a place of dubious legends and grisly deeds. Getting murdered in your bed was a regular pastime here, twelve in one night being the record to date.

Sleat is Clan Donald country. Like Armadale Castle,

the MacDonalds have seen better days. Once they were Lords of the Isles. The title reverted to the Crown in 1493 and is now shared between Prince Charles and a Calmac ferry.

Sleat has also become the hotbed of the Gaelic Renaissance, with local nobles occupying the roles of latter-day Medici and Borgia. At Ostaig old MacDonald had a farm and on that farm he had some students who have gone on to be big noises in the revival of Gaelic.

Bun Sgoil Sleite, the bi-lingual Primary School down the road at Kilbeg, is one school where parents don't complain about the language their children have picked up in the playground.

Pioneering Eilean Iarmain/Isleornsay is at the centre of these initiatives, as well as being the site of Skye's first public loo (which opened to a long queue in 1820). In past times otters hereabouts ravaged the locals' chickens; now each summer, at the quayside gallery, hens gather to kick sand in the faces of the superb stone otters taking shape under Laurence Broderick's hammer.

From Knock to Aird the coastline looks out to the Rough Bounds of Knoydart and to Morar with its white sands and twinkling camper-vans. When the raindrops ping off the windows of the boat from Mallaig, jovial visitors make witty and original comments about the name given to these waters, for this is the Sound of Sleat. It isn't, of course, for Sleat is pronounced 'slate' and takes its name not from the weather but from the word on the lips of those waiting on the pier at Armadale and muttering about the ferry.

Watch out for Sleat Fun Day in late July, the rest of the year being a time for sombre reflection.

STRATH

Strath is the next bit up from the bottom of Skye, from Kyleakin to Elgol. Strath is Mac-Kinnon country.

The south-east corner of Skye is different. There are fewer walkers. The reason for this is that, while the rest of the island is handsomely covered by OS Landranger maps for N & S Skye, territory here, together with large patches of sea not suitable for walking, belongs to Sheet 33, Loch Alsh & Glen Shiel. This costs £4.75 and is usually deemed not worth it, not just for that little bit.

Kyleakin is The Gateway to Skye. As with most gateways, people have now found a quicker way round to the side. The business communities of Kyleakin and Kyle, its other half, feel somewhat passed over by the bridge; but they have been given hanging-baskets to cheer them up instead.

Three miles up the road is the turning down Glen Arroch. From here single-track road winds its way for several hundred miles down to Kylerhea, where the otters hide.

WATCHING WILDLIFE

At the heart of Strath is Broadford, which is on the way to most places. Unusually for Skye, Broadford is the meeting-point of several roads; hence the ample parking, to accommodate bewildered visitors unable to decide where to go from here. Broadford has a wide bay, looking out over Pabay, rainbows and two piers, though neither has much in the way of seaside amusements.

From Broadford a narrow road leads west to Elgol, passing on its way the much photographed reeds of Loch Cill Chriosd and the even more photographed homes of Torrin. A large lorry pressing on your bumper at this point is a reminder of the presence of nearby quarries, famous for the Elgol Marbles.

Collections of cars in the middle of nowhere mark the starting-points of popular walks – along Strath Mor to Luib, up by the waterfalls to Blaven, over to Camasunary. Blaven was 'first' climbed in 1857 by a professor-to-be and a poet; for AC Swinburne this capped a lifetime of daring feats, done possibly to live down the name Algernon Charles. (Living dangerously was a habit with Swinburne. As an adult, he startled the Rossettis by sliding down the bannister of their home in Cheyne Walk – stark naked.)

Victorian Romantics went overboard for the wild scenery of Loch Slapin and who could blame them? Behind their backs in Strathaird, villages were cleared with a savagery all its own.

Kilmarie, pronounced 'Kilvory', takes its name from Maolrubha, an early winner in the competition for Celtic saint with the trickiest name to pronounce or spell.

For the 19th-century visitor to these parts, the highlight of the journey was the boat-trip over to Loch Coruisk. Turner came, equipped to capture in paint its watery atmospherics; Sir Walter Scott followed on, with a large bottle of purple ink. 180-odd years on, the same trip is still running – though, happily, not in the same boat. It's still the trip of a lifetime.

J.M.W. TURNER ON SKYE

1743 . THE LAST WOLF ON SKYE .

PORTREE

If they'd wanted the island's capital to be bang in the middle of Skye, it would have ended up half-way up Roineval (by Glen Drynoch) and without much to show for a harbour. Instead, Portree hugs sheltered waters and is as near to dead centre as dammit. If, at a pre-arranged signal, you released homing-pigeons from each of Skye's furthest points (Dunvegan Head, Waternish Point, Rubha Hunish, Kylerhea...), there'd be a nasty thud and a flurry of feathers, as they all hit the loft in Portree at precisely the same moment.

Originally called Kiltaraglen, Portree acquired its present name (meaning Harbour of the Slope) as a result of the royal visit in 1540. With its attractive quayside properties, Portree is often mistaken for Tobermory, especially by buyers of postcards.

Neatly laid out like a model town, Portree has one of everything: one hospital, one high school, one library, one fire-station, one swimming-pool, one lifeboat, one let's-build-a-new-high-school campaign, one Gathering Hall...and several million classy souvenir shops. Not bad for a village.

At the heart of Portree is a large square, built to accommmodate the queue for the bakery. Behind is the exclusive Park Lane area. This leads into Springfield, to be confused with Seafield, Bayfield, Viewfield, Hedgefield, Fisherfield and the playing field.

As capital of Skye, Portree is the starting-point for excursions and centre for tourist requirements. The Mountain Rescue Service, for example, is based in Portree, where it is frequently called out to lever apart climbers with rucksacks stuck in shop doorways.

AROUND PORTREE

All roads meet in Portree, all four of them.

Out to the north-west, the road passes Borve, where in former times the Nicolsons of Scorrybreac parked their carts and mustered their wagons.

South of Portree is the road down Glen Varragill, with a side-shoot roller-coasting off to the The Braes. Even better for your suspension is the Old Road to Moll, on the other side of Loch Sligachan. This is marked as the Scenic Route and brings you first to a quarry with industrial workings to gladden the eye. The next section has a surface maintained by the manufacturers of a well-known brand of travel-sickness pill. It is their test-route. In early summer there are foxgloves and roses at the edge of the road, which you can sit and admire while your stomach recovers.

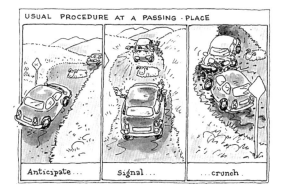

TROTTERNISH

With its fine walks, ace views and spectacular geology, Trotternish might easily be dismissed as much the same as the rest of Skye. But the north end is quite special, with sights arranged at regular intervals along the road which loops the peninsula.

First stop is by the Storr Lochs, which have a reputation for 'large and hard-fighting fish'. Above looms the Old Man of Storr, a mighty pinnacle of 160 ft, though it only comes out small in your photo. Up at the Storr Rocks, the Old Man is not the lonely figure he appears from below, but enjoys the company of other blocks and pillars that have been given the shove by the Ridge.

After Lealt Gorge comes Loch Mealt plus cliff-top viewpoint; from here anyone brave enough to look can see for themselves what is worn below the Kilt Rock.

Staffin looks out over two islands in a broad bay, while the Quiraing breathes down its neck. Traditionally used for hiding cattle, filming car adverts and hosting sports events, the Quiraing is a weird jumble of un-gentle scenery. Up behind the pinnacles is hidden the famous Table, where shinty was played (great fun if you were the one who had to go after the ball each time it went over the edge). To reach the Table means negotiating a steep slope, rained upon by things dislodged by visitors ahead. These may be small stones, medium-sized rocks or even large rucksacks, some with visitors attached. (These visitors are no longer ahead of you.)

> I suppose it was bound to happen some day –

FIGHTING FISH

There's more pinnacles to be found, this time rising straight out of the sea, at Rubha Hunish, the northern tip of Trotternish. Beside it is Duntulm, stunning at sunset.

The road bends south to Kilmuir, home of the Skye Museum of Island Life, which houses Flora MacDonald's egg-cup. Behind is the cemetery, where Flora MacDonald's grave looks out to her Uist birthplace and where the writer-traveller Martin Martin rests in peace beneath the Skye sky.

At Uig the road swings down to the bay via a hairpin bend occupied by people with cameras. If your vehicle goes over the edge at this point, rest assured that the moment will have been captured on video for your relatives, insurers and Jeremy Beadle.

On the opposite side of the bay is a round tower, known as Captain Fraser's Other Folly. (His first folly lay in his treatment of tenants, which brought about divine retribution in the form of the Uig Flood of 1877.)

Tucked in behind Uig is the Fairy Glen, a riot of manageable mounds and hollows for people whose legs go wobbly at the Quiraing. There are exactly 365 hills, arranged by the fairies into twelve little groups.

Somewhere round here is a secret underground chamber –

Off the road by Glen Hinnisdale is Caisteal Uisdean. Hugh's Castle (architectural style: Early Brutal) was the setting for events which might have come from a badly written opera. Deciding that the castle's house-warming would be the right occasion at which to have Donald Gorm (his clan chief and half-brother) bumped off, the gormless Hugh muddled the party-invites, slipping instructions for the would-be assailant into the envelope for his intended victim. The kind of mistake we all make. Instead, it was Hugh who was launched into eternity, dying crazy with thirst in the dungeon at Duntulm (the one with the lovely sunsets).

Visitors completing the Trotternish loop have just a few remaining ports of call: Kingsburgh (where Dr Johnson shared a bed with Bonnie Prince Charlie) and a choice of standing stones, by Kensaleyre, Borve and Tote. For enthusiasts, Skye has lots of stones, rather too many to list.

27

WATERNISH

Waternish (pron. 'Vatternish') is an attractive finger of land surrounded by vatter.

At its base is the Fairy Bridge, positioned, according to tradition, where three roads meet, three streams join and a camper-van sits. Further on, up by Loch Bay, is Stein, intended by Thomas Telford and the British Fisheries Society to end up like Ullapool. But the herring had other ideas. Stein remains as fine a spot as any from which to enjoy the sun going down through the base of a beer-glass.

Sober up by Ardmore and Trumpan, famous for ghastly massacres and fabulous views. These continue along the track through long-gone Unish and out to Waternish Point. On the way you pass a variety of Iron Age remains: two brochs, one van and bits of a Ford Granada.

28

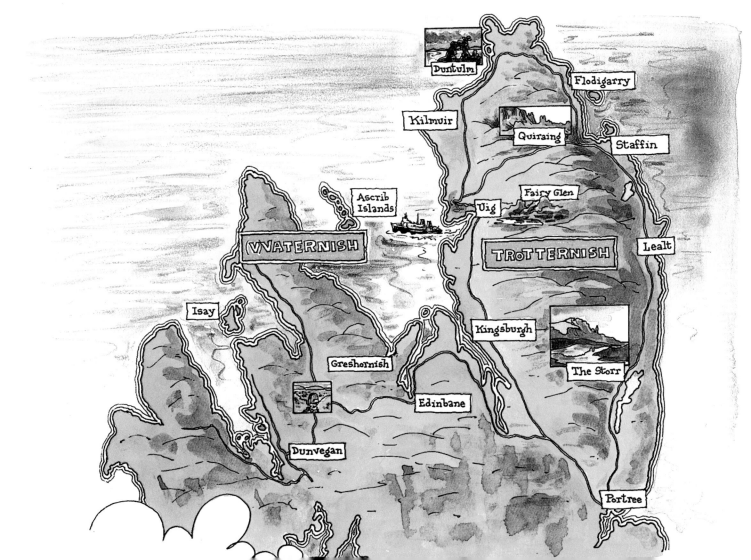

DUNVEGAN

Inhabited by 30 generations of MacLeods, Dunvegan Castle is reckoned to be the oldest property in Britain continuously occupied by the same family. Well, would you want to move after all that time? Just think of the amount of junk piled up over 700 years.

Something of a tourist trap, Dunvegan has been welcoming visitors for as long as any can remember. In the 1880s the author-cyclist 'Nauticus' arrived in Dunvegan to find himself invited by a visiting Yorkshireman to join him in a cup of tea. Presented with the following bill, Nauticus decided to cut short his stay:

	s.	d.
Tea	2	6
Washing hands	0	6
Total for one tea	3	0

Of course much has changed over the centuries. There were fewer coaches in Dr Johnson's time and the tea-rooms were on the other side of the car-park.

Inside the castle are many unusual treasures, including Bonnie Prince Charlie's hair and the glasses left behind by his pilot on the flight from Culloden.

Also of great interest to visitors is the false bottom in the Dunvegan Horn. The massive horn was hacked by the 3rd Chief from a wild bull which attacked him while out dallying (the Chief, not the bull) in Glenelg. Ever since, male heirs to the line have had to prove their manhood by draining in one go the five pints of claret it holds. (Note, claret not Scotch. Clearly not drinkers, the MacLeods.) Succeeding chiefs must at least be grateful that it was the horn and no other part of the bull's anatomy that Malcolm MacLeod chose as his prize.

P.S. Don't be too alarmed if, in the course of your visit, you happen to notice that the Fairy Flag has been temporarily removed from its case. This could just mean that it has been hoisted on the castle to encourage more herring into the loch. Or it may have been spread on a marriage-bed to encourage fertility. Or it's being waved outside to ward off a nuclear strike.

DUIRINISH

If the map of Skye resembles a set of unruly bagpipes, then Duirinish is the mouthpiece, the bit sticking out on the left. Duirinish is the Wild West of Skye, every bit as stunning as the rest.

The Tourist Route out to the West (there isn't another way) gives a glimpse of the Coral Beaches at Claigan, sizzling in the sunshine. Here the white coral (all right, seaweed) is lapped by gin-clear waters, complete with lumps of ice. At Glendale the Hamara River meanders in intricate loops, all but disappearing up its own bogside. Beyond lie Milovaig and the pier at Meanish, named after the forces sent in to put down rebellious crofters at the end of the last century. After trial and prison in Edinburgh, the Glendale Martyrs came home in triumph.

Neist is west and west is Neist and here the twain meet, in scenery out of this world. (Hell when it rains.) South of Waterstein, the road runs out at Ramasaig, leaving the walker to stumble on deserted villages and uncomfortable bits of history. Watch out for the ancient rowan tree, planted by homes in order to keep witches away. Very effective it is too.

The brochure did say it was basic –

Overlooking most of Duirinish are MacLeod's Tables (to be confused with Lord MacDonald's Table). The bigger of these is Healabhal Bheag (meaning 'small'). Healabhal Mhor (meaning 'big') is the shorter by 63 ft. The famous banqueting incident of the 16th century, from which they got their names, took place on one or other, depending on which authority you read.

If you look across Bracadale from Fiskavaig, you'll see there's really a whole nest of tables. And, if you have binoculars and know where to look from, you can even catch a glimpse of MacLeod's Maidens, discreetly waiting to serve.

There's a good laddie, run back down and fetch us more gravy –

MACLEOD'S BANQUETING HALL

COLIN BAXTER MEETS MICHAEL MACGREGOR

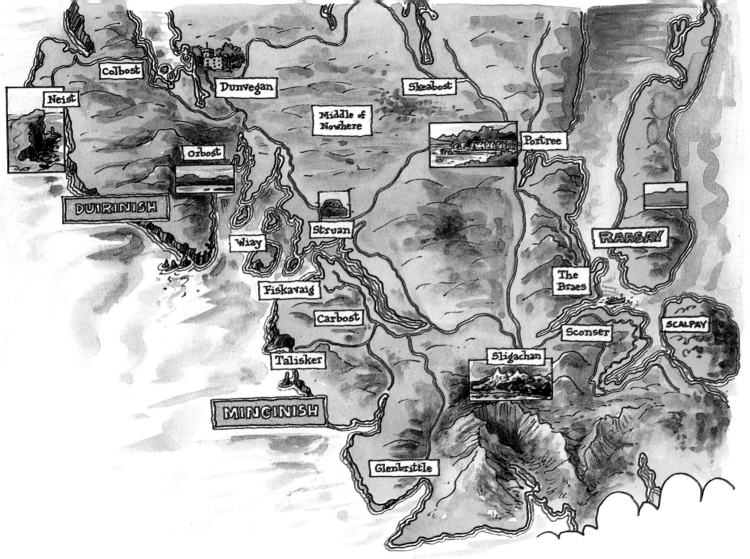

MINGINISH

Minginish has the Cuillins, Black and Red, linked and ranked like cards in a pack. Sgurr Alasdair is the Ace of Spades and Beinn na Caillich Queen of Hearts.

It's not new to point out that if Skye were Switzerland, the Cuillins would present a very different picture. Mountain railways, chair-lifts, cable-cars, tunnels, restaurants on every summit... and, right at the top, a little yellow sign pointing up into the clouds, saying 'Cafe/Sun Terrace – 15 mins'. And, if it were France, another little sign when you got there, stuck on the door, saying 'Fermeture Annuelle'.

Minginish also has Talisker Distillery, which attracts 40,000 odd visitors to Carbost each year – and plenty of normal ones too. Either way, it's a lot of hangovers.

I just can't get mine to curl like that, whatever I do –

Glens Eynort and Brittle are the main areas for forestry on Skye. (Lord MacDonald's Forest in Glen Sligachan is something of a disappointment.) But even these now face an uncertain future, thanks to the introduction of the plastic foam caber.

With beach on one side and mountains above, new arrivals in Glen Brittle are spoilt for choice of direction. One happy compromise is the walk out to Rubh' an Dunain, into scenery beyond compare. The coastal fort right at the end was long the stronghold of the MacAskills, who no doubt spent their days waving their arms at troughs and lows sweeping in from the west.

PROPOSED IMPROVEMENT TO 'BAD STEP' FOLLOWING VISIT OF HEALTH & SAFETY OFFICER :-

Falling body breaks infra-red beam activating...

..spring-loaded safety-net in fire-retardant material.

Skye High

IT was the Iron Age and had been so for ages. From the back of their cave, Mrs Thig stared out through curtains of drizzle at the jagged outline of distant mountains.

'Sping poddle tog?' she said (which translates as, 'Wot's them things called?').

Thig looked down at the recumbent whelp that snored in his lap. Its jaw hung open to reveal an irregular set of pointed fangs, out of which ran thin lines of bright saliva.

'Cuilean,' he replied (meaning 'young hound') and smiled at his joke.

* * *

Fearghus Og skipped over the sands, pointing and calling at the high mountains that reared over the loch.

'What?' he shouted. Or rather, 'Uamhthoirchoifhao-dhichuimhndhatharreachadh?', as it was in Old Gaelic.

Behind him, his mother stumbled on through seaweed and stones, roundly cursing the new-fangled Roman sandals she had bought just the previous day.

'More cheap foreign rubbish,' she said to herself, as one sole parted from its thong and the other wound its way up her knee. At that moment her foot landed heavily on a small piece of foliage that felt like a thousand needles.

'Cuilionn!' she screamed in not-so-soft Gaelic. 'Cuilionn-mara!' which is the Gaelic for 'sea-holly'.

* * *

As the Viking fleet drew level with Skye, 800 tired and homesick Norsemen dipped their oars and flicked back their blond tresses, pausing to admire the view. High in the helm, their leader, Bjorn, prodded the bundle of rags at his feet. It was Benni, in-board soothsayer and general know-all.

'Called?' said Bjorn, his arm outstretched toward the mountains.

The grizzled sage squirmed wretchedly in his bilge-seat. Through thick pebble-glasses he could just make out blurred grey shapes rising out of the sea.

'Kjölen,' he replied. It was Norse for 'keels'.

And the name stuck.

* * *

It's a funny old thing, coincidence.

Red Cuillin

THE CUILLIN(S)

Singular or plural, the Cuillin(s) is/are quite something. (Connoisseurs and Celts refer to them as Cuillin, beginners say Cuillins and others, as with this chapter, take a firm line, alternating strictly between the two.)

Identifying high points on Skye is not always easy. Sgurrs are peaks, beinns are mountains and anything else is dismissed as a molehill.

The mountains of Skye are colour-coded for your ease and convenience. The highest are black (except for Sgurr Dearg), followed by blue and grey (Blaven, Clach Glas). Next come the Red Hills (anything called Beinn Dearg) and, lowest of all, speckled or yellow (Beinn Bhreac, Beinn Bhuidhe). The system breaks down under snow or changes of light, which on Skye are constant.

THE BAD STEP

...as usually shown...

...as it really is.

BAD STEP

One of the best ways into the Cuillin is by boat from Elgol, but it doesn't get you up very high.

Alternatively, you can follow tracks from Strathaird or Sligachan. These entail squelching miles till you come to the insurmountable barrier known as The Bad Step. This cunning device is put there to separate sheep from goats. If the prospect of slithering off this slab into the icy waters of Loch Scavaig (all right, Loch nan Leachd) 30 ft below is something that turns your legs to jelly, here is where you look at your watch, peer at the heights, hum and hah and then announce it's probably time you ought to be turning back.

Black Cuillin

One way to avoid the Bad Step altogether is to do the Cuillin Ridge Walk. This is the great traverse, from Gars-bheinn to Sgurr nan Gillean (Glen Brittle to Sligachan). Seven miles, 40-odd peaks, 18 main summits, 14 of them over 3,000 ft; until 1911 it was reckoned by experts as impossible in one day. Nowadays it gets knocked off in under four hours. It can only be a matter of time before it gets done in less than three by somebody climbing backwards, blindfold and dressed as Bugs Bunny.

magnetic gabbro

THE RIDGE

THE INACCESSIBLE PINNACLE

41

MOUNTAIN GOATS

The magnetic gabbro of the Cuillin is ideal for climbers, offering challenges of every kind: cirques and aretes (circuses and bus-stops), ledges and chimneys, pinnacles and scree. All these are carefully graded in the climbing guides, from W (wimps) to DS (downright suicidal).

Conquering Cuillins is not everyone's cup of tea. The Inaccessible Pinnacle, for example, (or In Pin, as it's known to rock-jocks) is really not for the casual picnicker, as round things tend to roll off its top.

However, such is the popularity of getting stuck up mountains that many of the Cuillin's best-loved features are in danger of imminent erosion. Already the Bhasteir Tooth is down to 3,000 feet exactly and ready to drop from the list of Munros. The threat to Skye of having its jagged mountain outline worn smooth by the tramp of visiting feet is a serious concern, already being addressed by volunteer groups. Each Easter parties of students arrive with hammers to chip away at rounded surfaces and sharpen up the edges for the season ahead.

Watery Skye

Dolphins in The Minch

THERE'S a magic in the mixture of mountains and water. Scotland has plenty of both and Skye often seems like little else. Wherever you look there are high bits; wherever you step there is water.

The coastline of Skye has been teased out to maximum length, kinked and looped into sea-lochs and ragged with islands (most of them occupied at one time or other by Gavin Maxwell plus otters). Skye may not have the sands of Skegness or Bognor (try Harris), but neither does it have anywhere by the sea that stares out into the dull oblivion of a straight horizon. Coastal views here change all the time. Skerries and islets come and go; headlands and islands hove into sight, then vanish again. Really, they should be charging spectators.

ISLANDS

Land and sea fight for possession of the north in such a way as to make the map of Scotland look more like a drawing of Metamorphosis by Escher. Out west, only the bravest of dots (well done, St Kilda and the Flannans) dare put their heads above the waves. By the Western Isles, land is more in evidence, although North Uist still looks like a sieve, ready to submerge at any moment. Only by the time you get to the Cairngorms has land taken full control and water been left as puddles. The pattern is repeated on Skye, the west of which is basically sea with bits of land in it, while the east is the other way round.

The mountains of Skye crawl with outdoor types, all with *that* look in their eyes. These are Munro- and Corbett-baggers. Around the coast, too, there are obsessives, who have to set foot on every island. Let them on Skye. Just don't sit down on the bus next to one ready to reel off his list of conquests (it is always 'his', not 'her'). Scalpay, Pabay, Longay, Guillamon, Soay, Oronsay, Wiay, Tarner, Harlosh, Isay, Mingay, Clett, Ascribs, Lyndale, Fladda, Trodday, Flodigarry, Staffin, Crowlins…and those are just the bigger ones.

The name Oronsay comes from the Norse for 'ebb-tide island', which makes you wonder about Viking eyesight. Ebb-tide is the one time Oronsay is not an island.

He's exploring his roots —

42

LOCHS

… Snizort and Scavaig, Slapin and Brittle, Eynort and Ainort, Bracadale, Pooltiel and Harport. Not firms of dodgy solicitors, but wonderfully named sea-lochs of Skye, courtesy of previous invaders.

Inland (just), Skye has one famous loch (called Coruisk) and hundreds of little and not so famous lochs or lochans, usually called Loch Fada, Loch Dubh or Loch Mor (Long Loch, Black Loch, Big Loch).

Walter Scott was the first to go wordy over Coruisk and all writers since have tried to go one better, out-Scotting Scott in their passages of lonesome gloom and brooding desolation. The awesome quiet of Coruisk is enjoyed to this day by visitors on foot and there are plans for others to share in this by helicopter.

Seal culling

OTTERS

Otters are rotters. You can sit watching from the hide at Kylerhea till your eyeballs ache – and see lots of seals. You can stand in the gloaming by the shoreline, feasted on by midges till dark, staring at a rock that you could have sworn moved. You can even get to stay in a splendid B & B with a stuffed otter looking balefully down at you all night from its glass case on top of the wardrobe – and still never get to see the real thing.

But it's worth it all for that sublime moment when you do look down by chance from a coastal promontory to find a sleek and perfect otter, gambolling in the kelp at your feet. Truly a moment to savour, as the silvery bubbles rise from its dive and you whisper to yourself in awe, 'Bugger, I've not got my camera.'

WAITING FOR A BITE

Great – and now all close up a bit –

44

SEALS

The sea-lochs of Skye play host to a healthy population of seals. Some are grey seals, some are common seals and those bobbing up and down in straight lines are mussel-farms.

Identification of species is not difficult. It is a matter of deciding between common (or harbour) and Atlantic (or grey). The former are also grey and this is the Atlantic, while the latter are common and can be found in harbours. The grey (which is yellow at birth) is very variable in colour, from dark grey with spots through silver to brown, whereas the common, or brown, seal can be any shade of mottled grey or brown. The grey seal is described as having a distinctive dog-like head and the male is often dark with light blotches, while the female is light with dark blotches. The common seal, which is smaller (but not necessarily, depending on age) has a head more like a spaniel.

The best way to tell the species apart is by noses – one is snub, the other Roman. Nostril-types are completely different, except underwater. One is V-shaped, the other isn't.

The mating-ritual of the common seal requires the male to rise from the water, waggling his head from side to side with a large clump of seaweed in his mouth (one, perhaps, to try out first in the privacy of your own pool at home).

Regular boat-trips from Dunvegan, Kyleakin and Elgol enable visitors and seals to stare at each other from close quarters. The seals are well used to the click of the camera – some have gone on to pursue successful careers in modelling.

MARINE I-D CHART

| Minke Whale | Dolphin | Porpoise | Common Seal |
| Killer Whale | Grey Seal | Basking Shark | Calmac Tea-tray |

Natural History

BIRDS

HIGH in the moorland, where the air is thin and summer short, you may chance upon a circular patch of stubby, straw-coloured cylinders, looking as if some rogue motorist has chosen this spot to empty his ashtray. Closer inspection will reveal these to be not cigarette-ends but the visiting-card of a ptarmigan. The two are not hard to tell apart: ptarmigan droppings are difficult to light and give a much richer smoke.

With its unusual ability to change colour with the seasons, the ptarmigan can be a tricky bird to spot. Snowballs tend to fly straight; ptarmigan don't always.

drumming snipe

Ptarmigan in summer

I think it may have seen us –

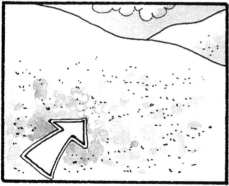

Ptarmigan in winter

A wing-span of up to 7 feet makes the golden eagle pretty unmistakeable, at least from close quarters. However, eagles are not easy to lure on to the bird-table, not unless you are into sacrificing large pets in a big way. Golden eagles are therefore inclined to remain distant and diminutive dots, which then turn out to be buzzards. These then turn out to be crows.

Eagles are always something special. It is not unusual to come across a car stopped in the middle of the road, its occupants leaping out with binoculars and pointing up into the clouds with cries of 'eagle'. This can puzzle continental visitors. 'Igel' (pron. 'ea-gle') is the German for hedgehog.

Wiped out in Skye in the early years of this century, the sea eagle is now making a controversial comeback. Re-introduced from Norway, the white-tailed sea eagle has upset local farmers by its choice of menu. While scientists work away at developing a new strain of bun-eating eagle, plans for the great bustard, the moa and the dodo have been put on hold.

The crofting meadows of the Hebrides are just about the last refuge in Britain of the once common corncrake, often mistaken for a fishing-reel. Find a hayfield on Skye and pause awhile. Place your ear to the ground and, if not by now on your way to hospital casualty with an eyeball speared by stubble, listen out for the distinctive 'creck-creck-creck' of the corncrake.

NB: learn to distinguish between the call of the corncrake and the approach of a tractor-mower.

Ptarmigan caught out
by a change in the weather

FLORA

Flora (i)

   See below, under Bonnie Prince Charlie.

   Flora (ii)

   Skye is blessed with a profusion of rare and interesting flowers, from Alpine gentians to insectivorous sundews that would have your leg off, given half a chance.

   There are several types of heather beside the standard ling: bell heather (which likes it dry), bog heather (which likes it wet) and lucky white heather (which grows near souvenir-shops).

Cirsium helenioides · Melancholy Thistle ·

MIDGES

Known and loved throughout the Highlands, the wee midge is a gregarious little chap, never happier than in the company of others. There are 36 varieties of biting midge in Scotland, but those on Skye are in a league of their own.

The Winged Isle

LIFE-CYCLE

Bred in captivity, midges are released into the wild at the beginning of the tourist season. Sunshine and visitors bring out the swarming midge in large numbers or 'gatherings', which are one of the great spectacles of nature. To be at the centre of one of these is usually a matter of patience and luck. (There is a wide variety of midge attractants available on the market.)

50

Midge·swats

Midges...

When summer warmth gives way to the first frosts, the midges return to their spawning-grounds to over-winter in purpose-built shelters. Bloodsucking is a female occupation – in the midge world it is the females that get lumbered with all the catering, while the males hang about in groups discussing the shinty

Midges can get out of hand and regular culls are necessary. Experiments with barrier spraying of DDT in the 1950s wiped out most known forms of life within the control area – except for midges, which had the wit to cling to the under-side of leaves, thereby avoiding the toxic sprays. Sterilisation of males is another form of control currently under consideration, but it is an operation that calls for keen eyesight and a steady hand.

Mindful of these difficulties, Forest Enterprise and like-minded authorities place large swats at the disposal of visitors in areas of high infestation.

Tourist Tip: watch out for local events run by the campaigning organisation SKRAM (Skye, Kyle and Raasay against Midges).

Highland Midge
enlarged (slightly)

Midges don't like wind. One development that visitors to Scotland may have noticed in recent years is the installation of powerful wind-generating fans on hill-top sites to combat the scourge of the midge in moorland areas.

① Belt & Braces

② High-Tech

③ Slow but effective

TRIED & TESTED METHODS OF MIDGE-CONTROL

History

S KYE has lots of history, most of it grim beyond words. Not having been flattened by harrow or housing estate, much of Skye's history is still strewn over the landscape and piled up at your feet. Archaeologists can have a field day on Skye.

The island's line-up of historical figures has a curiously back-to-front feel. The first known person on Skye was Artbrannan, who sounds more like an American business guru. The list comes up to date with the name of Robbie the Pict.

Back in the mists of time, when Artbrannan was out networking with clients, Scotland was called Alba and lived in by Celts like the Picts and Scots, who were Gaels and came from Ireland. People on Skye at this time lived in brochs, which were round towers by the seaside giving good views of hostile arrivals. Come the invasion, the locals could shut themselves up in their brochs and find they had no means of escape.

In 795 the Vikings came over the horizon. There followed 600 years of Norse invasion –one every summer with roads packed out and no room to move in the shops. Eventually some Norse families got fed up with all the travelling and came to settle on Skye for good. They were tired of the rat race and decided to find a quiet spot in which to set up a small business, making mugs and lampholders or doing unusual things with wax, leather and tin.

Following their away defeat at Largs in 1263, King Hako's fleet put into Bracadale to patch up their bruises, but then sank without trace in the Beazer Homes League of their day. This should have led to prosperity and peace. Instead there followed several centuries of clan warfare and general unpleasantness.

IRON AGE TIMES

53

GRISLY CHAPTER

This was the time when witches sang ditties on the heath and headless ghosts stalked castle ramparts; people with names like Black-Eyed Donald of the Bogs did unspeakable things to their guests and people with names like Ian the Ill-Fated did not sleep well in their beds.

Dunscaith Castle, grim and brooding, was originally MacLeod property, which was then overrun by MacDonalds, then swiped back by MacLeods, before being fought over again by different MacDonalds.

Knock Castle, also known as Caisteal Chamuis and also grim and brooding, went MacLeod/MacDonald/MacLeod/MacDonald/MacPherson. Duntulm went MacDonald/MacLeod/MacDonald/MacLeod/MacDonald. These were good times for the removal men on Skye.

Now a thing of the past, clan feuding stopped suddenly in 1595. That was when the MacLeods joined forces with the MacDonalds to set off for Ireland and fight against the English.By 1599 they were back at each other's throats again.

BONNIE PRINCE CHARLIE

The Young Pretender did Skye in just five days in the summer in 1746. He did have rather a lot of people chasing after him at the time and there were few opportunities for sightseeing in the course of his busy schedule.

Had it been Fred MacDonald, not Flora, who got him to Skye, or, perhaps, had he been Bonnie Prince Ronnie, things might have been different. But, as it stands, the story of Charles Edward Stuart's escape from Culloden could not have been bettered by Mills and Boon. It is one of the great tales of Scottish history – especially if you skip what happened next to the Highlands and Islands, after he had gone.

ANOTHER GRISLY CHAPTER

Culloden was, of course, the last battle fought on British soil. Another last battle fought on British soil was the Battle of the Braes in 1882. That was when Britain dispatched a gunboat to invade itself.

Both events took place on Skye and were part of the Crofters' War. On the one side were villagers wanting to collect driftwood, keep dogs and graze their sheep; ranged against them were baton-wielding policemen from Glasgow, constables from the mainland and warships with marines from Rosyth. No contest: the locals won hands down. Not that this was anything other than a hollow victory, after more than a century of oppression and clearance. Around 34,000 people were forcibly, often murderously, evicted from Skye, as the silent stones of Lorgill and the like so eloquently testify.

People

THE people you are likely to encounter on Skye fall into four broad categories – with every variation in between.

A) LOCALS

The locals (the true native *Sgiathanach*, born and bred) are often called Calum and Mhairi; they speak soft Gaelic and are very hospitable. Usually they work in computers, tend crofts and caravans, drive sheep, drink tea, take their time and wear whatever suits them.

B) INCOMERS

Incomers (sometimes known as 'White Settlers') often have children called Calum and Mhairi; they speak loud Gaelic and are usually very hospitable. Mostly they tend craft shops, drive battered Volvo estate cars, drink lots of whisky, take in guests and wear homespun things that occasionally smell of sheep.

C) TOURISTS

Tourists (sometimes called all sorts of things) are often named Gunther and Ingmar; they speak perfect English and tend unruly children in weather that's far from hospitable. As a general rule, they drive VW camper vans, drink something from a flask, take lots of photos and wear anoraks, capes and things that swish in shops.

D) CLIMBERS

Climbers are called Boggers and Jez. They speak rarely and sometimes end up in hospital. They tend nasty bruises and drive in tent pegs late in the night. Climbers drink like fish, take risks and wear dangly things about their nether regions.

THE WAY OF LIFE

Life on Skye is generally peaceable and law-abiding, ram-raiding and heresy being the commonest forms of crime. Sundays are quiet times, as are traditional rest-periods like Friday nights and Hogmanay. Visitors are requested to respect local sensitivities in such matters and to speak only in hushed whispers late into the following morning.

'...a quiet way of life.'

'generally peaceable...'

SKYE PILOTS

A word on religion: the Free Presbyterians (known as 'We Freeze') originally split from the Free Church (later united with the United Presbyterians to form the United Free Church), which originally broke free from the Church of Scotland, which had itself broken free from Catholicism.

You are welcome to join in prayers for Christian unity.

The call of the ptarmigan consists of 'croaks, squawks and a remarkably human belch...'

CLANS

Two centuries on from Culloden, the clans still play an important part in the Scottish way of life. Watch out for the demarcation signs by the roadside, as you pass from one territory to another (MacAlpine, Morrison, Tarmac, Docwra etc). In some areas Forest Enterprise goes one step further by planting out the countryside with lines of trees in the relevant tartan.

It is worth investing in a booklet on the subject in order to familiarise yourself with the attributes of each clan and to come equipped with the appropriate greenery. For MacLeods of MacLeod this is juniper, but MacLeods of Lewis should more tactfully appear bedecked in red whortleberry.

Aye, that's genuine, all right – I built it myself for the tourists.

Economy

SINCE the bottom fell out of the market for diatomite and kelp, you might have been forgiven for thinking that the economy of Skye could be summed up in just three words – crofts, crafts, Crufts.

Crofting is tough, especially for the womenfolk obliged to walk long distances with heavy creels of wet peat strapped to their backs. Not that digging up large acreages with a crooked spade is any easy business either. Instead much of the land is handed over to sheep.

60

A popular breed is the Cheviot, which can do things with its wool. The Blackface has a coarser fleece, suitable only for mattresses and carpets. Summer shearing is always a busy time, when extra hands are brought over from the mainland and swiftly deployed from place to place. If you visit in summer, watch out for the Shearings coaches.

Separating sheep from coats is laborious at the best of times. Scottish scientists are currently working on the concept of the self-shearing sheep, an idea almost as hard to envisage as it is to pronounce.

self-shearing sheep

' suitable for carpets . . .'

Tourism is the predominant industry on Skye and that has led to a re-birth of traditional skills, such as making batik and laser-printing of T-shirts. The boom in crafts has had quite an impact on the landscape. Such is the popularity of heather products for example (honey, ale and heather-stem jewellery), that large areas are now given over entirely to the growing of ling.

Long hair masking the eyes is still a much loved feature of the modern Skye terrier– that and a tendency to walk into lamp-posts. The breed is further described as having short, straight legs and close-set eyes (as far as one can tell), as well as a feathered tail, which is unusual in a dog.

Colouring varies from light sandy to dark grey and even blue, if it gets that cold.

Sturdy, alert and relatively weatherproof, the Skye terrier has a double coat, with tough, glossy top-coat overlying an insulating undercoat (but no primer). Hair length has long been a bone of contention. Back in the 1860s, Captain MacDonald of Waternish, a noted breeder of short-haired Skyes, stormed out of the Inverness Dog Show when the judges gave first prize 'to a whitewash brush'.

The long-haired Skye terrier shows a certain nervousness (which is understandable) in the presence of dustpans and buckets of whitewash.

SKYE TERRIER

It was Queen Victoria who made the Skye terrier fashionable. Small and dumpy, with a large head, low body and powerful jaws, the Empress of India knew what she liked in a dog. With its sombre colouring and distinctive veil, the Skye terrier was an obvious choice for the queen.

Skye Terrier

Whitewash Brush

63

TALISKER

One of the most popular visits on Skye is to the Talisker Distillery at Carbost. Visitors (who must pay) are welcomed in with a free dram before embarking on a carefully guided tour around various obstacles. The trip through the distirelly ends in the distillerelly shop. Here visitors can invest in a choish of items unique to the Talishter Diskillery on Stye, before driving off into Loch Harport.

Talisker has a seaweedy nose and a memorable finish.

The image of Scots
as hard drinkers
is of course only a myth,
borne out by statistics.

Parting view of Talisker Distillery.

How to Serve It:
Scotch on the Rocks

64

Visiting Skye

FOOD

VISIT any shop in these parts and you swiftly realise how restrictive have been the effects of poor access and harsh climate upon the feeding habits of the Highlander. People here live mainly on oatcakes, shortbread and fudge, leavened only by clootie dumpling.

Good Food campaigns are bringing change. Seafood is increasingly chic – local seafood so fresh you wonder just how it gets away with it. More and more restaurants are turning back to traditional dishes of the region – such as colworts, brochan and oon (foaming milkfroth) – in place of the ubiquitous salmon and venison in wine.

Distance and weather have given the region something of a reputation for soft fruit – don't hesitate to complain if the produce which reaches you is not crisp or fresh and in the peak of condition. On Skye itself, for many years now, extremely high standards have been kept up by catering establishments, fearful of the sudden appearance of Derek Cooper.

Pride of the local cuisine is its baking – delectable scones and buns, such as those to be had from MacKenzie's Bakery in Portree. (MacKenzie clan motto: I shine, not burn.)

DRINK

Talisker is not the only fine liquid to come out of Skye. MacLeod's Isle of Skye whisky (made in Edinburgh) is a blended Scotch, using Speyside sophistication to tame any gauche tendencies in the raw spirit of Skye.

Drambuie (also made in Edinburgh) also originated in Skye, from the sporran of Bonnie Prince Charlie, to be precise. Short of loot with which to reward his post-Culloden protectors, the Young Pretender was reduced to handing out culinary tips. MacKinnon of Strathaird was the lucky recipient of the recipe for Drambuie ('The Isle of Skye Liqueur'). His neighbour had to make do with how to deal with awkward soup-stains.

A recent development has been the setting up of a whisky company in Sleat. Poit Dubh (pron. 'potch ghoo') is a vatted malt which is Gaelic-speaking. Te Bheag is a blend, pronounced 'chey vekh' by those who know and 'tea-bag' by those who don't.

Over at Uig, meanwhile, award-winning ales are produced by the Isle of Skye Brewery, Leann an Eilein ('Lean on Eileen'). Red Cuillin is smooth and rounded, while Black Cuillin has more of an edge.

Red Cuillin ... ..Black Cuillin

THINGS TO TAKE HOME

One of the great success stories of recent times has been the traditional Isle of Skye tartan, devised by a Lewis man and marketed since 1992. The soft hues of purple and green are designed to blend in with the colouring of visitors' knees when temperatures drop. A new kilt can be pricey. If you're out of pocket at the end of your stay, the same attractive design can be found in wrapping-paper. However, this is much less hard-wearing, especially on damp ground.

One popular souvenir is the local midge bite, sported by many a traveller homeward-bound. Go for the full set and impress your friends. (These won't last for ever, of course; expect some signs of fading after a few months.)

Even less long-lasting is likely to be a bottle of Talisker, one of the six Classic Malts of Scotland. Insist on checking the sell-by date, together with the strength (a heady 45.8% alcohol – neither more, nor less).

KEY TO COMMON SYMBOLS IN TOURIST PUBLICATIONS:

Telephone not connected

Damp picnic spot

Bring your own lightbulbs

Nothing on television

Watch out for short measures

Beware - line dancers about

Inquisitive pig loose on site

Careful what you step in

English not spoken

Some paths can be muddy

Sewage outfall nowhere near

Be prepared for mauling by owner's dog.

Put that back this instant!

WHERE TO STAY

Finding somewhere to stay on Skye is not usually a problem. Indeed, the island has so many B&B places that for much of the summer, during the breakfast hour, large parts of it disappear beneath the morning haze produced by frying-pans filled with bacon and eggs.

Accommodation varies – from caravan to castle, plush hotel to bunkhouse, bothy or byre. Don't assume that all will have the same mains services available to you at home and do watch out for the Thistle sign, denoting comfort.

Getting About

SKYE DRIVING

ONE piece of motoring equipment to invest in is a large white flag. This is for waving at critical moments, such as seconds before impact. Better still, position a flagpole through the sun-roof of your vehicle and train those in the back to hoist the flag from your well-judged hill-top passing-place, while you await the cautious approach of the vehicle spotted from an earlier ridge (and now also in long-term parking, awaiting your approach). Single-track roads are a common cause of misunderstandings, except for elderly residents whose gift of second sight enables them to know what is round any hill or corner.

Never saw a thing –

It's the way they just shoot out from the side of the road without any warning –

70

For those new to the system, a clear set of rules exists for single-track roads:

i) give way to buses, lorries and travelling salesmen.

ii) do not use passing-places for overnight stops, as the tent-pegs leave nasty little holes in the tarmac.

iii) keep a careful eye out behind for local traffic needing to get past. Should the registration letters AS (short for Angry Scot) appear pressed against your rear window, it is only natural courtesy for you, as a trundling tourist, to take an immediate nose-dive into the heather. Off-roading has a big following on Skye.

iv) do not argue with sheep or Skye Marble lorries, especially when fully laden.

v) should you encounter a fire engine on its way to an incident, you should, of course, reverse at full speed the whole length of the single-track road.

vi) when two vehicles meet midway between passing-places, it is the one going uphill which has priority. Thus, a coach heading down to Elgol should reverse up Blaven until the lone wobbling figure on the mountain-bike has managed to get by.

vii) when two vehicles meet midway between passing-places on a level section of road and both drivers are of similar age and gender, priority is established by the toss of a coin, the drawing of straws or whatever other method of reaching a fair decision is agreeable to both parties.

viii) get to know and use the recognised signals:

a single flash of headlights means, 'Thank you for waiting – I'm on my way' or 'All right, all right, it's not worth arguing over, but yet again I seem to be the one stuck waiting.'

a double flash means, 'Come on, you nerd, I'm not waiting all day' or 'Have it your own way, Prawnfeatures, but just don't try stopping me now.'

a triple flash, followed by a loud bang, means, 'I suppose we'd better exchange insurance details.'

Some day we must get ourselves a proper little runabout for these afternoon drives out with your mother –

As ever, courtesy is the keyword to success. Motorised vehicles are still something of a rarity in Skye and the tradition continues whereby drivers acknowledge each other with a raised finger or hand, depending on the warmth of the salute.

This can be tiring in built-up areas and it is possible to buy a small device which, at the touch of a button, presses a plastic finger to the windscreen. Some gadgets have the facility for raising a second finger, should the need arise.

PUBLIC TRANSPORT

Lots of people come to Scotland for the walking – which is just as well, in view of the infrequency of public transport. Skye, by contrast, is rather well served by buses, although you may begin to think differently, if you're the one standing at a bus stop. There are five different companies competing for your custom. And if none of them show up, you can always send yourself through the post, without even needing a stamp.

Post-buses operate around Elgol, Glendale and Waternish. Happily, passengers are not charged according to weight, although it can be cramped waiting in a pillar-box.

FOUR-LEGGED FRIENDS

Police clampdown
on stray animals

Despite regular police crackdowns on their activities, stray sheep can be a problem. The tendency of local livestock to set up roadblocks in unexpected places is something to watch out for. Keep your speed low and driving licence handy.

Sheep give way to gentle persuasion. Cows give way to nothing on earth. Even on Skye, a discreetly executed 73-point turn and general decision to go somewhere else may prove quicker than trying to get past the bloody-minded creature that's blocking your way. Lone cyclists should keep in good physical trim and be prepared to lower the angle of their handlebars to something less provocative.

Do not be tempted into using the damp fleeces of roadside sheep to give your car a much needed wash 'n shine. The sheep's revenge is to turn tail and decorate your vehicle instead with an interesting pattern of greens and browns.

Tourist Tip: before leaving home, fix an 'I'm a Real Scot' sticker to the back of your car.

CYCLING

Cycling around Skye is a form of ordeal increasingly popular in recent years. It is not unusual along the roads to meet a hairy-kneed cyclist pounding ahead, with thighs like pistons and smoke coming out of his bottom, followed several miles on by a tight-lipped spouse, grimly pedalling. Some people try tandems instead.

WALKING

The first rule of walking in Skye is to remember that water flows downhill, except in Scotland, where, the higher you go, the wetter it is. Waterproof footwear is a must in Skye.

WATERPROOF FOOTWEAR IS A MUST ON SKYE...

ORONSAY

Never venture out without the right equipment, even when tempted only to make a quick dash for the shops.

Scotland does not have the same harsh laws of trespass as exist south of the border. Instead, intruders are shot at with high-velocity rifles.

'unrestricted access to the countryside'

Chapter Eleven: GETTING ABOUT

'COME ON, YOU LOT — NEARLY THERE NOW!'

In the right season, walkers can enjoy unrestricted access to the Skye countryside, but novices are best advised to stick to well-trodden paths. Classic walks include the climb up to the Old Man of Storr (only the fittest need go right to the top), the scramble up to the Quiraing, the ramble down to Camasunary and the long hobble across the car-park to the medics in Portree, to see what can be done about that ankle.

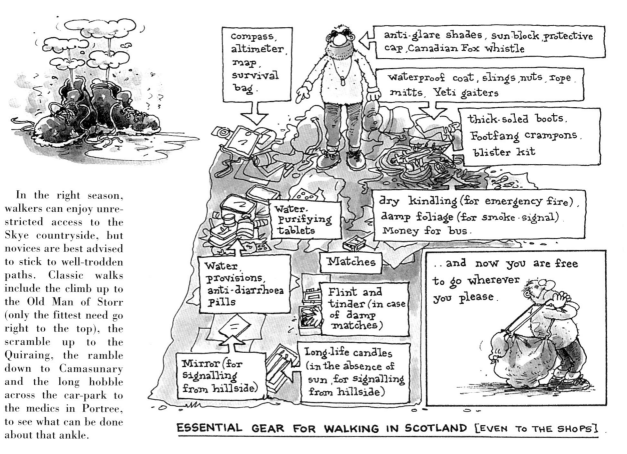

compass, altimeter, map, survival bag.

anti-glare shades, sun-block, protective cap, Canadian Fox whistle

waterproof coat, slings, nuts, rope, mitts, Yeti gaiters

thick-soled boots, Footfang crampons, blister kit

Water. Purifying tablets

dry kindling (for emergency fire), damp foliage (for smoke-signal), Money for bus.

Water. provisions, anti-diarrhoea Pills

Matches

Flint and tinder (in case of damp matches)

..and now you are free to go wherever you please.

Mirror (for signalling from hillside)

Long-life candles (in the absence of sun, for signalling from hillside)

ESSENTIAL GEAR FOR WALKING IN SCOTLAND [EVEN TO THE SHOPS]

well trodden paths ...

However, not every walk need push back the boundaries of human endurance and fitness. There are plenty of pleasant strolls to be had in the softer hills and glens, many of them remarkably soft. Nor need every route be uphill and vertical. The walk from the Storr Lochs to Bearreraig Bay, for example, is downhill all the way (between six and seven hundred steps, depending on how many times you lose count). As is so often the case in Skye, getting back is more of a problem.

HEADGEAR NOT SUITABLE

FOR WALKERS IN THE SCOTTISH HILLS

Apparently this is an old drove road —

Most walks on Skye begin with a fine, clear path, which then divides and sub-divides like crazy (courtesy of vindictive sheep), leaving you with a choice of several hundred paths, all of them ending in bog.

To help out those stuck in the said bog, there is plenty of helpful advice (look out for the guide to guidebooks on Skye). Beware of those describing walks as 'suitable for any footwear'. Some of those moorland tracks can't half mess up your best stilettoes.

Those who know a thing or two about Skye are the ones who set off from their cars in thigh-length waders with sun-protective hat and ski-sticks. You just don't know how fast the weather may change in Broadford.

Follow the distinct grassy footpath for the next 2 miles...

Sport

THE Big One on the sporting calendar is the Highland Games. These take place in August in the perfect setting of The Lump, purpose-built by nature. The games attract a huge crowd into Portree, there to enjoy the deft skills of pipers and dancers, skipping to avoid the battery of large objects hurled at them from very close range. As popular as ever are the traditional manhood-proving contests in weight-throwing, caber-tossing and extracting your car from the car park.

999? No, it's the TV series with Michael Buerk that I'm trying to get through to –

THINGS TO DO

Skye offers riding, canoeing, golfing and fishing in the fast-flowing rivers and inland lochs. Pony-trekking centres on the island employ the traditional breed of nimble-footed and sturdy Highlander – and the horses are quite special too.

Water-sports fans can take part in windsurfing, kayaking and canoeing, all giving a taste of local waters.

For golfers, the 9-hole course at Sconser is filled with challenging possibilities. A wide slice on to the Raasay ferry, for example, would land you at E. Suisnish, from where it is a long drive back on to the fairway at Sconser. A second course exists at the Skeabost House Hotel, at the head of Loch Snizort. An early visitor to this spot was St Columba of Iona, though history does not record whether or not he brought his clubs.

There is excellent fishing to be had on Skye, owners and fish permitting. The lochs have brown trout, the rivers have salmon and sea-trout, and the sea has seals, which swipe the lot.

If sitting in the rain for 18 hours leaves you cold, there is always the Glamaig Hill Race to consider. This takes place in July, emulating the feat of Gurkha Thapa in 1899, and is run more or less from the front bar of the Sligachan Hotel up to the top of Glamaig and back again. It takes around 44 mins 41 seconds. Add 17 hours, if not wholly fit.

Glamaig Hill Race

FLY FISHING

FLY FISHING:
first catch
your fly...

THINGS TO SEE

Clan warfare down the centuries, over and above the sheer struggle for survival, denied Highlanders the conditions necessary for the expansion of leisure activities. For many a long year, the glens rang out to the crunch and clang of weapon on skull. All that is happily now a thing of the past. They play shinty instead.

Combining the best elements of hockey, golf and tree-felling, shinty is a traditional village sport, well-rooted in Skye. Played with long sticks and usually a ball, shinty is much the same as Irish hurling, only differently spelt. The two games are similar enough for Shinty-Hurling Internationals to be held either side of the Irish Sea – an idea that has yet to be taken up with Europe by devotees of, say, pétanque and bowls or bullfighting and rounders.

Football, too, is popular on Skye, with a keen following for local teams like Glasgow Rangers, Portree, Dunvegan, Celtic and Strath & Sleat.

SHINTY TEAM - Back row (l to r): Donald 'Cross' Macleod; Donald 'Legs' Macleod; Donald 'Kojak' Macleod; Donald 'Datsun' Macleod; Donald 'Two Feet' Macleod; Donald 'Nip' Macleod; Donald 'Sausages' Macleod; Donald 'Bealach' Macleod; Donald 'Pardon' Macleod; Donald 'Ginger' Macleod.
Front row: Donald 'Loud' Macleod; Donald 'Stan' Macleod; John 'Donald' Macleod; Donald 'Erk' Macleod; Donald 'Duck' Macleod; Donald 'Eigg' Macleod. (Absent from photo: Donald 'Gone Again' Macleod.)

WHAT'S ON

Dog trials, classic car rallies, gala days, agricultural shows…there's always something happening on Skye, at least from May to September. Many a full day ends with a night on the township.

In June, for example, there is Gala Day at Elgol, complete with slave-auction and biggest slob competition – for anyone who can be bothered to go along. August has Portree Show, with juggling goats, log-sawing, sheepshearing, races and similar events put on by local livestock. The Dunvegan and Kilmuir shows also give visitors a chance to see sheep.

And then one day in Autumn, at a pre-arranged signal, when the last lingering tourist has left the shops, suddenly there is a rattle of shutters and snatching in of signs, one huge collective sigh of relief and Skye is closed for winter.

Then it's time to hang up kilt and sporran and settle down to all those out-of-season jobs – like re-harling the porch, polishing the Bad Step and deflating the seals on the loch.

SHEEPDOG TRIALS

The Arts

MUSIC

WHEREVER Gaels meet, there is music. Be it formal gathering, impromptu ceilidh or chance encounter in the launderette, out come the fiddle and accordion, clarsach, pipes and drums. They love a good sing-song in Scotland.

Skye is, of course, the home of bagpiping. For 300 years, on the north-west tip of Skye (and just out of earshot of Dunvegan) the MacCrimmons taught piping at Boreraig. Even the MacArthurs (hereditary pipers to the chiefs of MacDonald) came to learn from the MacCrimmons (hereditary pipers to the chiefs of MacLeod). *Piobaireachd* brings people together and friendly rivalries are re-kindled each year in ferocious competitions for both chanter and quaich.

SKYE BALLS

Alive and kicking, Skye music caters for all tastes – from Peat Bog Faeries and Jabble down to opera and classical recitals. Celtic Rock has a huge following, thanks to bands like Runrig, who have done so much to rock the Skye boat. And, for easy listening, there is piped music in the larger hotels and public spaces.

A happy forcing-ground for younger talents is provided by the regular festivals and mods arranged in different venues, upon which performers, press and scooters then descend. The National Mod in October is a great occasion for artistes to come together and squabble about things.

They like a good sing-song in Scotland

OPEN · AIR THEATRE :

That's midges they're clapping –

PORTREE IN MOTION

Many visitors take one look at Skye and are smitten for
life. Skye Fever is an incurable condition. Time was
when the worst cases were shut away in institutions.
Happily we live in a more liberal age. The old Skye
Fever Hospital, on the edge of Portree, has been closed
down and turned into an Arts Centre instead.

With its galleries, workshops and open-air theatre, An
Tuireann is a place for people to come and strike sparks
off each other.

VISUAL ARTS

Skye's stupendous scenery and quality of light attract
artists from all corners – that and the desire, having
escaped from the south, to find some way of making a
living other than by collecting winkles.

JMW Turner was one of the first among many to find
inspiration in Skye, developing an impressionistic, wet-
on-wet approach to Loch Scavaig. Since then, countless
artists have sought to set up their easels on the island,
making it something of a latter-day Arles or
Montmartre, only with fewer nude models.

The Gaelic

GAIDHLIG, PRON. 'GALLIC', AS IN 'PHALLIC'.

LEARNING Gaelic is not as difficult as it looks.It's considerably worse. Hats off to those who can speak it, especially from birth. Having the Gaelic is not something you achieve in six weeks, with the help of one slim volume and ten tapes. Allow 30 or 40 years, at least for the grammar, and a similar period for pronunciation. No wonder it nearly died out.

If that seems harsh, try these for rules:

☐ a feminine noun in the nominative case aspirates the adjectives following.

☐ if no 'i' is present in the final syllable of a plural noun, you have the unlenited form of the adjective.

☐ a present participle taking a noun object requires this noun to be in the genitive case.

The Gaelic alphabet has just 18 letters. There is no J, K, Q, V, W, X, Y or Z, which makes it a dead loss at Scrabble. However, the remaining letters are put together in every conceivable combination, with an 'h' interspersed, which then makes preceding consonants silent – sometimes. The result is very long words, which trip off the native speaker's tongue with beguiling ease and leave the learner howling for aspirin.

The little midge, for example, becomes in Gaelic A' Mheanbhchuileag. The name Norman translates into Thormaid, pronounced 'Horrormidge'. Cameron becomes Camshron, pronounced 'Cammaron'; but Portree, spelt Port-righ, is 'Porsht ree'.

One recent development has been the spread of bi-lingual signs (Mol/Moll, Sligeachan/Sligachan, Scullamus/Skullamus etc). These have done much to make Gaels feel more at home and to save visitors from getting lost in places they cannot pronounce.

An attractive way into the language is via the place-names and local topography. But there is a limit to the conversation that can be had with Black Rock, Red Burn, Yellow Hill...

Unable to achieve full fluency in the course of their stay, many visitors go for the easier route, dropping a few well-chosen words from the vernacular into their speech ('aye', 'wee', 'the noo'...) in order to be better understood by the locals.

A' Mheanbhchuileag

Gaelic symbol

A few useful words and phrases:

Gaelic	pronounced	English
smuid-uisg'	smooj ooshk	drizzle
lon	lawn	puddle
tea	tea	tea
bog	boek	soft
snog	snock	pretty
carabhan	swine	caravan
's math sin	smashin	that's great
cheery	tchee-ery	cheerio

TIGH BEAG

Trans:

* I don't understand

** What did you say?

THE WEST HIGHLAND FREE PRESS

The Free Press is a publication like no other. Set up to knock the Establishment, it is now an institution in its own right. A paper with a record of speaking its mind and not minding what it says, the WHFP is there to ruffle well-groomed feathers.

Inside, instead of the usual run of motoring offences, incest and burglary that brighten the pages of weekly regionals, there are donnish dissertations on events from past centuries and learned pieces on herbal cures

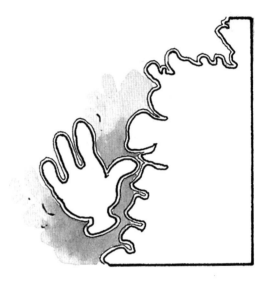

for dropsy and warts. No doubt they're right: the recovery of Gaeldom is big news and not just for Scotland.

Also inside: venomous letters, lashings of sport and an ace cartoonist, at whose feet yours truly grovels.

Tourist Tip: The West Highland Free Press is not free. It costs 49p.

The Neighbours

NORTH-EAST

THERE'S not much to the north of Skye – just the North Minch and then the North Pole. A hundred miles or so out from Flodigarry are the lone skerries of Sulisker and North Rona, on which the inhabitants of Trotternish depend for shelter when the wind blows in from the north.

East a bit and down a bit come Cape Wrath (from *Hvarf*, the sound on Viking lips as their boats rounded on the swell) and Sutherland, notable for its many peaks named after famous racehorses.

Coming into sight of Skye is Wester Ross, with Gairloch close enough on a clear day for its residents to look into the front rooms of houses in Staffin. (Staffin folk are far too discreet to peer back.)

Moving on down, the heights of Torridon and the wilds of Applecross rise up over Rona and Raasay, before dropping into Loch Carron. Tucked into this corner is Lochdubh, formerly Plockton, but now generally known as Tannochbrae/Ballykissangel or just Thatplacewheretheydidthatthingonthetellyyouknow thatonewiththedogandthecowinthestreet.

For one moment I thought that was a 'T'!

RAASAY

The sound of Raasay is the chuckle and plink of moorland streams, rising over the murmur and hum of bees in the heather and broken only by the soulful squeak of a Raasay vole... Actually, the Sound of Raasay is stuffed with nuclear subs, plumbing the depths.

Raasay's high point is Dun Caan, the peak of which was flattened in 1773 after being danced upon by Boswell. The views from Dun Caan are of a sort to make the spirits sing. But not the spirit of the sabbatarian Mr MacFarlane who, in the 1890s, sought to ban poetry, music and dance. As campaigns go, it wasn't that successful: in 1911 Sorley Maclean was born on Raasay.

Skye Terrier on the trail of a Raasay Vole.

Getting from A to B on Raasay was never that easy, especially when A was Arnish and B was Brochel. The story of Calum's Road has passed into folklore. Never mind if he did get a helping hand along the way, Calum Macleod's ten-year toil to build the road that the council would not provide is the stuff of legends. (He got through two wheelbarrows, six picks, six shovels, five hammers, four spades and one half-crown book of instructions along the way.)

If you get that far in the car, roll down the windows, sup in the views and treat yourself to a hum-along fortissimo of Capercaillie's tuneful tribute, *Calum's Road.* The only other vehicle you're likely to meet is another nutter out doing likewise.

P.S. Best not do this on a Sunday.

P.P.S. Check your fuel before you go: Raasay's filling-stations are back on Skye.

Dun Troddan

SOUTH-EAST

Beyond Raasay lie the imaginatively named islands which make up the Crowlins: Eilean Mor, Eilean Beg and Eilean Meadhonach (Big, Little and Medium Island).

Around Kyle the mainland enfolds Skye in a bear-hug of beautiful places: Balmacara, Kintail, Dornie (generally known as October, November and December on Scottish calendars). Kyle itself is the gateway to Skye, as well as home of BUTEC (British Underwear Testing and Evaluation Centre).

Glenelg, another gateway, is famous for candles, brochs and its welcoming inn, with shyly retiring landlord. Mallaig, another gateway, is a busy fishing-port, where seagulls dare.

Knoydart has one brief stretch of road, starting and ending nowhere (sorry, Inverie), which is ideal for learner-drivers with access by helicopter.

From Knoydart to Moidart, and on into Ardnamurchan, it is wild and unspoilt: the only sounds to break the silence of the glens are the roar of a stag and the trumpeting of fifty-something executives from the Home Counties, sent out in the rain to learn leadership and corporate bonding.

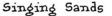

Singing Sands

SMALL ISLES

Largest of the small islands surrounding Skye are The
Small Isles, some of which are very big. Rum (the 'h' was
lost about the same time Peking changed its name), Eigg,
Muck and Thingy – or Muck, Eigg, Canna and Wotsit –
are collectively known as The Small Isles (or
'Rumeiggmuck' for short).

Eigg is the one with bits sticking up at either end and
Rum is the one that also sticks up, but more so; Canna's
the one around the corner. Or possibly Muck. Usually
one of them is hidden from view, but it's hard to remember which.

Eigg, now happily bought by itself, is the one that's
been in the news lately, over several decades. Rum
doings in nature conservancy also sometimes hit the
headlines. Canna and Muck keep a lower profile.

STAG AT BAY

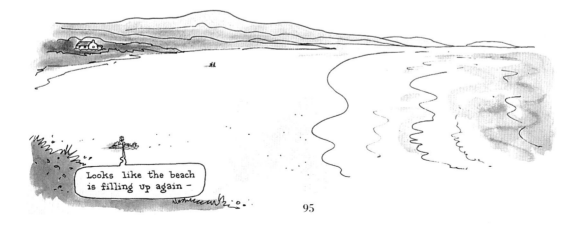

Looks like the beach
is filling up again –

OUTER ISLES

To the west of Skye lie the Outer Isles, and beyond them is sweet Rockall. No one coming to Skye who has ever watched the sun dip down behind the Western Isles could not wish to leap on to the next ferry from Uig to visit those magical places. But that's another story.